# — CULVERTS —

## BENEATH THE NARROW ROAD

# — CULVERTS —
## BENEATH THE NARROW ROAD

## BRENDA SCHMIDT

*thistledown press*

Thistledown Press Ltd.
410 2nd Avenue North
Saskatoon, Saskatchewan, S7K 2C3
www.thistledownpress.com

Library and Archives Canada Cataloguing in Publication

Schmidt, Brenda, 1965–, author
Culverts beneath the narrow road / Brenda Schmidt.

Poems.
ISBN 978-1-77187-154-9 (softcover)
I. Title.
PS8587.C45588C85 2018      C811'.6      C2018-901132-7


Cover and book design by Jackie Forrie
Author photo by Harvey Schmidt
Printed and bound in Canada

Canada

Canada Council
for the Arts
Conseil des Arts
du Canada

SASKATCHEWAN
ARTS BOARD
cultivating
the arts

Thistledown Press gratefully acknowledges the financial assistance of the Canada Council for the Arts, the Saskatchewan Arts Board, and the Government of Canada for its publishing program.

# Acknowledgements

Thank you to all the people who engaged with and contributed so generously to this project. Select answers to interview questions are used anonymously and creatively in this book and appear in italics. Thank you to Dennis Alm, Leroy Alm, Wayne Alm, Vernon Andres, Courtney Bates-Hardy, Annette Bower, Jared Clarke, June Danngren, Michael Deal, Gerald Hill, Crystal Kolt, John Lent, Carin Makuz, Suzette Mayr, Courtney Olmstead, Judy Pettersen, Pearl Pirie, Nick Sali, Harvey Schmidt, David Sealy, Glenda Walker-Hobbs (with thanks to Harry Hobbs). I am so grateful.

Thank you to Dionne Brand, Greg Cook, Sylvia Legris, Garry Thomas Morse, and Mitch Spray for valuable culvert-related conversations. Thank you to the amazing Garretians for comments on early versions of some of these poems. Thank you to Ariel Gordon, Tracy Hamon, Barbara Langhorst, and Bernadette Wagner for ongoing creative support. Thank you to Kathie Alm, Madeline Alm, and Marilyn Petersen for always being there.

The books *Seed Catalogue* by Robert Kroetsch, *Dart* by Alice Oswald, and *14 Tractors* by Gerald Hill were important influences. It was Gerald Hill who gave me a copy of Matsuo Bashō's *The Narrow Road to the Deep North and Other Travel Sketches*. Thank you.

Thank you to the Saskatchewan Arts Board for the grant supporting the creation of this work.

Earlier versions of some of this work appeared in the *Society, Canadian Poetries, The Best Canadian Poetry in English 2015*, and *The Best of the Best Canadian Poetry in English*, Tenth Anniversary Edition (2017), and was part of the "Wall of Miracles" poetry installation at the University of Exeter, UK. Thank you to the editors.

The opening epigraph is from *Idaho Winter* by Tony Burgess (Toronto: ECW Press, 2011). Used with permission of ECW Press and author.

The epigraph for "A Culvert and its Reflection" is from *Jacob's Room* by Virginia Woolf. Edited by Flint (2008) 16w from location 1820 (ebook version). By permission of Oxford University Press.

Thank you to Michael Kenyon for editing this book with such great attention and care. What a fabulous experience. Thank you to the wonderful people at Thistledown Press for bringing this work forth.

As always, thank you to Harvey Schmidt, the first reader of my work, for everything.

What a tremendous journey this has been.

# CONTENTS

*She was being carried down the river by the current and people just started following her cries. Along the river into an open culvert. Underground. To here. We live here now. With her.*

— Tony Burgess, *Idaho Winter*

## The Culverts Beneath the Narrow Road
## Through the Deep North and Other Travel Stretches

"What do a culvert and the Nobel Prize in Literature have in common?" I put this question to H as we approach the pair of culverts near the Manitoba-Saskatchewan border five minutes into our drive home from Flin Flon, our car packed with gifts and Christmas goodies for the big trip south. He doesn't blink. Of course he doesn't. Nothing I say surprises him anymore. He knows better than anyone how difficult writers can be to travel with, due in part, perhaps, to sensory overload, all these places flying by, all these junctions, private roads and keep-out signs, the mind filtering the 100 km/hr stream of information for connections, no matter how tenuous, to its own stories, untidy narratives typically ongoing and unresolved. Place a difficult writer in the passenger seat, throw in the weight of the holiday, a slow zone, and the questions begin well before you hit the border.

The culverts beg for such questions, sitting as they do. Large and black, likely made from some type of plastic, the two let water flow under the mine service road, or at least one does. Shortly after installation they began to acquire the same rust-coloured bottoms that gave their steel predecessors such character. While they both should be cuddled in snow, the rusty bottom of the culvert on the far side is exposed.

> bondage gear
> with icicle
> spikes

"I give up," he says, but I'm sure he knows, as he absorbs everything. Maybe he isn't replying to my question. The answer, I tell him, is Alice Munro.

The far culvert failed a couple years back thanks to a flood, I think, and now it points upward at the same angle as the Air Farce chicken cannon. That comparison dates me, I know. I don't know what causes the rust. This morning, like most winter mornings, a crowd of cattails wearing toques of snow stands next to the culverts, so the water quality can't be too bad, though I have no idea what cattails can tolerate. Their stems might carry the rust all the way up to their heads. I can almost feel the fuzz as we drive by. On days this cold a cattail feels like a lint brush, but the temperature is expected to rise ten degrees by midafternoon. Stroke it then, eyes closed.

> the velvet
> dress I
> wore
> as a girl

I press my forehead against the side window and picture Alice Munro doing the same, her forehead melting the frost, her eyes taking everything into the darkness to send it forth with a rush into the light. Such brilliance. I've been thinking about her a lot since she won the prize. Imagine what she could do with this place. The off-kilter culvert, the road with the arm to keep us out, the mining complex beyond, the smokestack standing there, too much Viagra.

> top of the Canadian
> Shield
> curves
> are covered
> with the usual
> lofty
> snow

It doesn't get much sexier than that. Come to think of it, the failed culvert appears aroused, too. Culverts might be responsible for the rising birth rate. It's easy to plant ideas in people's heads when they're driving home, hungry and ready for bed.

Culverts require regular attention. If a culvert becomes plugged with debris or dammed by beaver, if it collapses, the road will wash out. Alice Munro knows this. The culvert appears partway through her story "Runaway" and was maintained by a poet. I tell H this as we pull into Creighton, drive by our house, but that's not where we are headed.

the house faced
our passing
with a cool neutral
expression

"Makes sense," he says: "Who else?" True. Who but a poet would bother? I don't tell H about the young couple in the story. Their lives a mess, their fantasies about the poet disturbing. It's too early in the day for that.

I read the story last night before we set out, though I can't say why it keeps returning to me or why I make so much of the culvert. Did Alice Munro have a specific culvert in mind when she wrote it? But of course now it's an everyculvert into which we direct the flow of our lives. Sitting in a pub in Regina once with a group of friends, some from larger cities, I mentioned I was installing a culvert. "I don't know what the hell a culvert is, no offence," said one (she was as brilliant and well-educated as it gets).

storm grate and sewer
more a passage through
a rat-infested unknown

In the context of Alice Munro's story, the meaning of "culvert" is clear, unmistakable, but in a loud pub, the burning fireplace beside us, our hands reaching for nachos, the cheese pulling thin and letting go, the word made no sense, nor did it matter.

I remembered the culvert in the ditch I played in when I was a kid and proudly scooped up some salsa.

I don't know what the hell a culvert is, no offence. I suspect her words still bother me because after all this time I don't know either. It's easy to use the word as a noun, but touch an actual culvert, or experience a culvert, the noun feels all verb, all flow. It feels like hell. It feels like an offence. It's undoubtedly offensive. It's night, all the rats I've known staying hidden. The need to enclose whatever wells up or courses through is overwhelming, the impulse to channel everything into *an image*, contain whatever you can't face, tame and make respectable — all this is both instinctive and dangerous. In the car my mind repeats images of the numerous culvert failures in Saskatchewan caused by heavy rain a few springs back. I'd never felt so uneasy. Everywhere the ditches were full, the culverts hard-pressed to handle the flow. Safely north, I became obsessed with news reports of the disaster unfolding in the southern part of the province. Concerned about the wellbeing of my family, worried about their flooded basements, worried about the future of their farms.

> I was looking
> down on a self
> truly haunted

> All that roiling
> water turned
> a thousand acres
> into swamp

Culverts broke loose and shot downstream with the force of the torrent. Culverts held their ground stoically. Roads disappeared around them and people stood at the edge, looking as if their whole world had washed away.

Culverts hold all kinds of positions. A friend's son was conceived in a culvert. We were sitting with a group in a backyard when he shared this piece of information. It was happy hour and I'd just told him that I had yet to meet someone with whom to share my love. I guess I asked for it.

> a huge culvert
> sun striking
> the steel

dragonflies
zipping by
its mouth

My friend's big feet sticking out, heels up.

On our way to Swift Current a good decade ago, travelling through the landscape of my youth, we came upon a section of highway under repair, a new steel culvert beaming on a bed of lush grass in the ditch. "Stop," I said. And there was no escape. H stopped. There was no one around, nor could we hear any vehicles coming.

the swish of wind
the song of horned

larks
the crunch of footsteps

H stretched his legs. Through the ditch we went.

As soon as I entered the culvert I realized you can't compare a new uninstalled culvert to one that's been in the ground for a while. With no sediment to blanket the bottom, the steel ribs protruded like those of a starving cow. The thrust of sun bouncing off the corrugated steel was psychedelic. Each step hit me with an echo. I plugged my ears, banged my elbows. When I turned, H was watching quietly from the opening, smiling at my awkward passage, but he made no effort to join me.

The same smile has followed me to Creighton this winter morning. Us and our little questions. The frost doesn't seem to be melting. I point the vent at the window and try to focus on something other than Alice Munro and that story, but I dwell on it. I dwell on it now at the stop sign where H turns right and heads down Main Street. It's as quiet as you might expect on a day this cold. On the way out of Creighton, I notice

fox tracks
lead to a lone

culvert in the tailings
pond dike. Unlike

the pair on the other
side of town

this culvert is small and placed high up the slope. I tell H to stop.
He pulls over without question. I get out. I squat to better frame the
blue shadows, shadows that become more purple the lower I get. The
hazard lights click like heels. "Runaway."

my breath
rises

matching
the dance of steam

from the mining
complex

on the far side of the tailings pond. I take a picture of that too. I have
it. Then I get back in the car and we carry on.

# A Citizen Scientist's Life Cycle

*In summer the culvert didn't seem so mean, just dried up like everything else.*

1.

Pulsing darkness. A chorus without pause
issues forth from the culvert's mouth
as it does throughout the year, spring flows
peaking now, beating me and the metal both.
A bit dramatic perhaps, but that's me
these days, feeling my age, my crooked toes
digging at my boots like gophers fleeing
too late the strychnine found in their burrows.
The colourless and bitter can make life
one long convulsion, a violent rush
from end to end. I hear the half-
crack of my knee, wonder who in the bush
will note the trudge, the hunch, conduct yet
another survey. Just me, I bet.

## 2.

Another survey. Just me, I bet,
here in the ditch, listening for owls.
I set the timer for two minutes, forget
tick by tick as timed minds do when strict rules
demand stillness. Hearing the click of crowns
in the wind brings shivers. Black spruce are evil
queens in this light, or Baskerville's hounds
gnawing the wet hollow in which I dwell.
The alarm sounds. Then a long staccato
from the east, as if blood-crazed gundogs
are cheering the hounds on. God only knows
why an owl sounds like this, or why my legs
nearly buckle on impact, like a deer
gut-shot, heading for cover, the bluff near.

3.

Gut-shot, heading for cover, the bluff near:
life is a passage and here I am, prey
preying on fear. A hunter always fears
the animal inside that waits for the day
it reveals itself. A spring bear, hungry,
slow-hearted, ambles toward the bacon
grease and fish guts, chocolate cookies,
the spot I fail to scrub off my hands.
Standing here, I am bait. The smell lingers.
I am drawn to it as usual.
Down the road, I'm told, a trail cam captures
passing deer, the odd coyote, vultures, all
in black-and-white, like any memory.
I squatted there last week. Too much coffee.

4.

I squatted there last week. Too much coffee
shakes my grip, the camera, makes images
blurry, the spruce grouse a brown streak. Sorry.
Believe me, the red combs above its eyes raged,
almost burned me, almost set the forest
alight. That's right, it was early morning,
I hadn't slept and the dew was less
heavy than the fog. There was no warning,
no calling, and I didn't see the root
over which I tripped, nor the crossing,
nor the culvert, though the sound trickled through
my ears. Weary, I heard something passing
close by, swore it was my soul taking leave
and there it was, a grouse in the leaves.

5.

And there it is. A grouse in the leaves
uncovers the unfashionable
Romantic, so rural and lost. I wave
at my own reflection, pull the wool
tight around my neck and shiver at how
old the ripples make me look, how tired
I am, lame, trying to walk like Thoreau
and my Thoreauvian friends. A liar
must do much better than this, be much
more than a body given to pauses
to search through the field guide for a match.
The Latin name of this bird amazes
naturalists no end, so I'll act astonished
until I believe I'm astonished.

6.

Until I believe I'm astonished
I will stand here and suffer. I promised
myself I'd be more awake, attuned, pushed
aside branches, woods and ruins, but a mist
has settled in the low spots like mist does.
Spring is beautiful. I use beautiful
too much, more than allowed, just because
petulance contains a single petal,
and that's enough to bring forth the flower.
It blooms. A curse, this lack of subtlety.
Like the marsh marigold, it's pure
poison. That nectar summons flies and bees
and me! Things grow cruel in the perennial
surface runoff, the ephemeral pool.

7.

Surface runoff. The ephemeral pool.
Call it what you like. I'm up to my boot-
tops in snowmelt, up to my ears in fools
who go on as if nothing else could suit
this April night. Perhaps the frogs are right
for here I stand in the cold among them,
too human to be any good, midnight
pressing certain stars into my brainstem.
It's calm now. The Big Dipper handles breath
gently, turns and washes it. True. The grave
forest covers up every little death
with another. I die a bit each day
behind this mask. The heart freezes and thaws,
pulsing darkness. A chorus without pause.

# A Culvert and its Reflection

*A raft of twig stayed upon a stone, suddenly detached itself,*
*and floated towards the culvert . . .*
— Virginia Woolf, *Jacob's Room*

Clearly caught in upsetting reflections,
Unable to determine the course, gold
Leaves drift aimlessly over swallowed stones,
Vanish just like that . . . This is getting old.
Endings float and bob into the half-stopped
Rusted chamber. Hello? Sure, spiral ribs
Trouble the passage. Hard to say what slipped

Through. What stayed? A mess, that's what. Up for grabs
Really means your tight grip on a dark past
Encloses the light as well and such light
Varies so. You can't blame the waves. The worst
Leaves eventually. You wait and wait
Until the twigs again let go. Some rafts
Carry piles of sharp sticks. Those are the gaffs.

## A Nice Halloween

1.

*It was a nice Halloween. We were in town tricking. I was fifteen or
sixteen. Some old bachelor was shooting at us with a pellet gun. We put
a culvert across the road so the cops couldn't get us. It was just sitting
in the ditch. They chased us on foot. P hid in an outhouse. The cops got
him. I phoned Dad and he came and picked me up at the post office.*

2.

It was Halloween. Nice to be done, I say as I hand over the keys.
What a nightmare: shift change, post-shift post-mortem, the death
relived on the cold walk across the parking lot. Shifts like this
are never over. You only live once, they say, but that's just wishful
thinking. You repeatedly limp toward the flashing amber hand.
Wasn't it here that I last saw the undertaker? But lights are lights
and now here he is, and here I am, both in vehicles, idling, him
heading east and me west, both waiting for the light to turn green.
How many bodies have we turned and moved from bed to stretcher?
How many times have we split the weight? The sun is in his eyes. He
doesn't see me. He has both hands on the wheel. So do I.

3.

It's Halloween! Let's go to the social. If we hurry we'll get there
before last call. Already loaded, I grab a garbage bag from under the
sink, slit a hole in the bottom, one in each side, and over the head it
goes. Butcher twine for a belt seems fitting for a short shift. Nice.
Not as thick as a shroud, but black is flattering. Five minutes later
we walk into the social. The music pounding. Some drunk throws
me over his shoulder and turns to leave. "Time to take out the
trash." His buddy flicks a lighter.

4.

Nice Halloweens are a thing of the past. Now they're about waiting.
This year I am in town with the lights off and the blinds down, a
bowl of chocolate bars by the door just in case, but no one knocks,
and in fact not one kid has knocked in years, so I try a bar. Still
cold. The chocolate bears a white film and tastes salty. At nine
o'clock I take the bulk of the bars back downstairs and bury them in
the freezer under a whole salmon, though it seems wrong to call it
whole when it's missing its head.

## The Culvert Between the Punishment Fields

*I'm stuck in the fuckin' thing!*
*Crawled in and got stuck.*
Couldn't move forward
couldn't move back.

The odds were good
he'd pull himself through,
small as he was,
but got shoulder-wedged

or maybe tired,
afraid of the way
the steel ribs wrapped
rust around his own. The dim

light ahead winked
whenever he breathed,
the underworld smelled
beer on his breath.

A child nearby later dreams
questions are trackhoes
digging up the road, a crew
with visors, torches cutting

through steel: How long
can a soul last without water?
Is that a dime
under his tongue?

## Just Rotten

*At first it just looks like a short tunnel but once inside I really like the portals.*

Today a warming hut called
The Hole Idea is sinking
through the ice into the Forks
where the Assiniboine
meets the Red. You can't
make this stuff up, you'd have said.

Rivers want rivers, frozen
or thought, the heart a mere hut
in which we pound and shiver.

Though small, the CBC image
shows the taut line from the yellow
warming hut to the tow truck is all
that keeps the Looney Toon
design from sinking farther.
There's no skating around this,
you'd have said.

Look
the ice between us is rotten.
It's now more

than a month since
the deep radio voice announced
your sudden passing,
the private service
already past.

Steel blade strikes steel
wall and here we are.
Is that a chain or a rope?
you'd have asked. Is this a time
of holding or pulling?
We both know

there's more than one
way to be cold while sinking.
Look, you'd have said, those two
grey ropes of smoke
in the background
behind The Hole Idea
aren't attached to anything,
still they meet. No wonder
breaking under the weight
the ice wets itself. Rotten
luck, you'd have said, cracks
a rotten heart. We're in this
hole now. Right now
I'd have you say anything.

## That Feeling When

*The culvert was still.*

eyes open
you can almost feel

lashes lift
the dust

that settles on each filament
you're pushing fifty

upside-down
the shoulder harness

holding you inches
away from the roll cage

chin
holding the whole

weight of the cherry helmet
a hanging basket

from which your hair falls
like a prayer plant

the tendrils of friendships
have come to an end

with blue sky beyond
and you suspended

this is what happens
when you whip the Odyssey

around in a summer
fallow field

you're not sure
how to right yourself

so much
pressure on the belt clasp

people
running and yelling

don't move
as if you can

or can't feel
your legs or your feet

# Thirteen Ways of Looking

*Beavers stuffing the irresistible sound of running culvert in their 7th line*
*pond.*

I

Look here, through
the eye of the blackbird
and not just any blackbird,
the rusty blackbird
suggests as it struts
through the mud
near the mouth of the rusty culvert.

II

Speaking of rare birds,
dear Wallace,
I think of you now
that the walleye are running
through the culvert
the way your eye once did
not so much across the page
as through it. Not that we call
them walleye here.

III

That said, I think of you
only rarely. Another spring
on the Shield and my
one mind is on that. The rusty
blackbird has disappeared
in the deadfall
which has disappeared now too.

IV

Winter has pushed more trees
into the water and once
again the beaver
shoves them down
the culvert's throat.

V

Wind south at twenty.
The stiff-lipped
culvert is the only one
whistling here.

VI

The moment
a sucker
bellies up
to the rusty
belly of the culvert
I suck mine in.

VII

The wind has picked up.
The culvert howls
at the water.
Ripples, wrinkles,
same same.
Tell me, what's twenty
like again?

VIII

Tail slap *ker thump*
culvert answers back
hard rock fist bump.

IX

Look. I believe
the rusty culvert longs
for spring like the rest of us.
And for the rest of us
for that matter.
Look! Here it comes!

X

Was it worth muddy boots
to get here?

The mouth of the culvert
opens up.

Sores on its lip.

XI

Branch cum barge
with buds attached
as always.

The past is the pass
you make at yourself.

Wait,
is that a leech?
To leech its own!

Not funny.
But you laugh anyway
as always.

And through the culvert
it goes.

XII

A sucker
bellies up
to the rusty
belly of the culvert
where the sucker
that went belly up
now bobs and rots.
The rusty culvert issues
a conditional discharge.

XIII

Waiting for the rusty
blackbird to return. Waiting

for the rust to return
the culvert to its former state.

## So Much at Stake

*Once I tucked into a culvert, its wide corrugated stainless-steel wave cool
and rough on the finger. Just room enough for me with knees folded to
chest. My jean pockets lumpy, full of the newest pretty stones. I didn't
want to sleep in case a freak storm came and drowned me.*

Today an eagle
circling over
a backroad
bump sign leaning
back in the snow
near a culvert
reminds me
of a picture
I saw yesterday
of you, friend,
on a beach
at an all-inclusive
resort drinking
a margarita I think
through a straw
red in the face

eyelashes
in a tired dihedral
diamond
flashing in the sun
a warning maybe
a promise that
the surface can't be
trusted yet.

## An Old Family Recipe (passed down by a master)

1 hot afternoon
1 *most practical brother*
2 close friends, of course
1 box of empty beer bottles
1 old *tank top* you never want to see again, torn
1 jerrycan of gas, freshly siphoned
1 box of REDBIRD Strike anywhere matches

1. Fill the bottles with gas.
2. Stuff each one
with a strip of shirt
torn edge out.
3. Each strike a match.
4. Hold the match to the shirt
5. Once the shirt catches
aim for the top
of the culvert.
6. Let go with force.
7. Repeat.

# Elegy

*At dances people hid their booze in culverts. We'd go back and swipe
their 40s.*

I'm not good at this.
I'm not good at anything
that involves looking back
at the meltwater slowly
filling in my boot prints.
I can with some small
degree of comfort
tell you that even though
it's April the forest still
holds onto the snow
that fell when he left us
and beside me the paw
prints of a wolf still
contain cubes of ice
and over there a whiskey
jack calls for calm in the willow
and you can tell it knows
no one will ever know
where it's nesting.

## Let's Try This Again

*Those were the days of no ear protection. He said that sometimes if the holes didn't line up he had a hand punch and a sledge hammer and one guy was on the outside and one guy was on the inside. Can you imagine?*

The moon, I think,
beginning, bent over
the bard like it is
right now, all alone
and not wanting
company. It's happy
hour somewhere
or so my friend says.
The moon nursing
another cold one.

## Two Day

*The culvert at the end of our lane heard most of our family's stories.*

A two-year-old
wearing a giant

pair of rubber boots
hauls a green two-

gallon watering can
onto the street and there

between the ditches
waves bye-bye.

## O Lorne

*There's a little Lorne Culvert in all of us!*

That's an inside Saskatchewan joke and not too dirty considering
you were our leader. Though you're not really a Culvert,
Wikipedia does point to a former ministry and rural congregations,
suggesting, at least to me, the draining matter of dwindling faith.
Have you noticed how full the ditches are these days?

What I mean to say is, I can relate. I swear, by my own name,
every Christmas at least one of my new and democratic friends
will think of me when they see an angry Santa yelling at Rudolf.
O the Schmidt house punch line again! Ho ho ho. Sure it stinks, yet
have you noticed how we're privy to the outflow of joy?

## Culvert Jazz

*it's a kind of magical hidey-hole*
   a sound hole
the ditch a soundboard
     pick guard  saddle
bridge  the whole
   instrument
vibrating from pin to head

*and it's got great acoustics*
   so you fret inside  solo
the strum  the pluck
     the plunks
press into the licks
   the ridges  the soul pluck
the steel back

*if you have a guitar with you*
   rest it on your belly
go with it  they say
     fretwork is gut work
it comes to you
   straight from strings
pitched a certain way

## Riveting

*The first ten-foot culvert I put in was in Herbert. There was a wooden
bridge there that the municipal guys were trying to blast. They couldn't
get it right, so I set the blast because I had worked in the mines in
Northern Ontario and I knew how to blast.*

000

July 1, 2015. A cliff swallow pops up in my Twitter feed and glares
at me with its right eye. Its head is trapped between the index and
middle finger of a man's hand, the claws of its feet digging into the
man's ring finger, the bird ready to spring from the palm should
the fist open. The swallow looks both afraid and defiant. The tweet
accompanying the image tells me the swallow was caught in Herbert
and you can tell it expects to die there at any moment.

*The steel came in at nine feet corrugated flat, then put in a roller, cut in lengths we needed. Then we riveted them together. You punched a hole, put the rivet in circular and lengthwise. First there were two men doing this job; one guy ran the machine and one put the rivets in. You had to make sure you didn't get your fingers in the machine.*

ooo

I know the biologist holding the swallow, so I email him. I was in Herbert in late June doing research on a large culvert about a mile outside town under a piece of the old TransCanada, just off the main highway, following up on information from the person who had installed it in the early 50s. I have a snapshot of him on the bulletin board beside me. His daughter sent it to me. She's the reason I drove to Herbert. In the picture her father, dressed in jeans and a black and red jacket, dark cap and black-rimmed glasses, is standing beside a long shiny steel culvert inside what appears to be a large building, light pouring in the three windows on the far wall well beyond the wood beam that stretches across the top of the picture. Near the centre, a vertical post rises and in front of it, perhaps attached, a green and yellow machine with giant yellow pulleys or gears and an array of hoses stands many feet higher than the man. A stack of rolled corrugated steel waits behind him. I can't see his expression, but his body language says he's relaxed and happy to be there. His posture is impeccable. I ask the biologist if the cliff swallow was part of the flock that was nesting in that culvert. Yes, came the reply, it was.

*The last time I noticed a culvert was Feb. 10, 2014 on Highway 11 on the way to Saskatoon from Regina near Blackstrap Mountain resort. Noticed it because I remember being there when it was installed in the 1950s. We stayed in the town hotel. The bathrooms were down the hall. Sometimes there were four men to a room or two to a room. It was summer. It took about two days. We put the culvert together there. It was a multi-plate bolted together.*

ooo

It turns out they captured twenty-nine cliff swallows at that culvert that day, all adults, all of which had taken to the sky and swooped down at me just weeks before when I skidded in my runners down the ditch to the creek edge hoping to get some shots of the nests. Cliff swallows regularly nest inside large culverts. Each nest has one hole. It serves as both entrance and exit. But the water was too high, and the swallows kept swooping, clearly disturbed, so I quickly took a few photos of the outside of the culvert to prove that I was there, then crawled back up the ditch, crawled in the car, and left. It's the multitude of pellets, I now think, the mud bound to mud bound to culvert, tiny heads peeking out of holes, that pulled me down that steep incline to peer inside the culvert.

*When I hear "culvert" I think about being under the railroads and roads.*
*We'd dig and then jack the pipe in and jack and again dig. Imagine sitting*
*in a thirty-six-inch culvert digging out the dirt and sending it out on a sled.*
*Only one guy could sit in and work. Usually we were only two feet under*
*and trucks on the road were driving over us.*

ooo

The biologist said no young were seen flying around that day, so
they assumed that they hadn't fledged yet. Not a biologist, I assume
that young love drives the birds to build their elaborate gourd-
shaped nests on the inside of a culvert, a culvert put together by
a man whose love brought forth a daughter, a daughter who now
creates romances herself, and here I am partway through her novel,
driving the old highway, a minor character in an unfolding story.
Meanwhile, just feet beneath my tires, cliff swallows are squeezing
out one speckled egg after another.

*Once when we were at St. Joseph's Colony it started to snow so we drank wine in the culvert and put a canvas over the power plant. A fire started and we burned the whole power plant.*

ooo

This was the biologist's first attempt to capture these birds. They plan to monitor this site as well as another culvert close by for the next five to ten years.

*I think about all the places I went and I went to a lot of places people don't even think about. Even stayed in farmhouses when working under a big trestle for the railroad.*

000

August 6, 2015. My blog feed tells me my mentor, originally from Herbert, has published a post on his blog titled "On Assignment For Brenda Schmidt's Culvert Project." In it he reveals that he too has talked to the romance novelist, a mutual friend, about the culvert's history. Also, somehow he has managed to take a photo of the inside of the culvert, capturing the nests. "I'd already announced several years ago that I want my ashes scattered along here," he writes, referring to that strip of old highway. I picture cliff swallows of the future scooping up mud and sticking to the culvert bits of the skull that kept my mentor's mind in place.

*In the winter we stockpiled. We'd make just about a mile of pipe a day.*
*We also made steel for steel buildings and tunnel liners.*


ooo


Sometime between August and before they return to breed next
spring, the young cliff swallows will do a complete body moult, the
biologist tells me. That means all feathers will be replaced.
I don't tell my mentor that I've been to see the culvert; I'd been
there before him. I don't tell the romance novelist either. On August
18, she comments on my mentor's blog: "Dad is surprised to see a
picture of the first culvert he installed."

Cliff swallow feathers are falling.

*Our building was close to the railroad tracks and we'd go out with a sled and load the steel onto the sled and pull it back to the shop.*

ooo

I imagine mist nets block both ends of the culvert, but I don't know this for sure. I imagine the cliff swallows swoop, get caught up, handled, weighed, banded, and let go. I imagine every swallow watches every capture and the captured look into the camera. In the coming dark, nightmares of feathers fill the muddy gourds.

*Before 1953 we rolled a lot by hand. In 1953 we got a crane and that crane is still operating. In 1954 we got a forklift.*

000

June 4, 2017. A cliff swallow pops up in my Twitter feed and glares at me with its right eye. Its head is trapped between the index and middle finger of a man's hand, the claws reaching up and digging into the man's index finger, the shadow of the claws on the nail of the man's middle finger. The swallow's leg band looks like a tiny culvert.

# Summer Job

*Use a trackhoe. Have to use the one with the thumb on it. Lower your culvert in. Load of dirt, packer, load of dirt, packer, load of dirt, packer.*

The east end of the grid seems the right place to start. White shorts, thin terry. Orange tube top. It couldn't be hotter. Horseflies bounce off my legs. All the heavy equipment is gone. Gone is the scraper, the driver. I choose the north ditch. I must handpick what the rock picker missed. I didn't think there'd be so many. Rocks the size of baseballs, whiskey bottles, the neighbour's head. All rocks over a certain size have to go for the road to pass inspection. It feels like I've been here forever. I bend towards the storm that's building in the west and grab another. Before I straighten up, I look between my legs. Look at all the rocks I missed.

# A Culvert Blown into Four Pieces

1.

*The low side of the street*
for those who know the real
meaning of low and high

*ran past our place*
perhaps the only place
that truly matters

*to a giant culvert*
though what giant
means is sometimes in doubt

*at the north end.*
As opposed to the south
of cottages and holidays.

*Even the most*
with the least always close by
to allow grudging comparison

*daring among us*
usually a few steps ahead
all the while looking back

*would not approach*
for approach births the worst
kind of caution

*that culvert whose blackness*
matched the spine barely holding
the songbook together in church

*told us*
in whispers
at night

*we were goners*
and by golly
the going wouldn't be pretty.


2.

*So in spring melt*
and spring keeps
coming and coming

*or after a rain*
which, like love
comes less and less

*we'd float our boats*
race our boats
from that day on

*down that stream*
for that's why a stream
ends with "m"

*toward the culvert.*
The culvert against which
all others will be measured.

*No boat*
as we will determine
over a lifetime of such thoughts

*was much of a boat*
for no boat
ever is

*(a toothpick*
spared a visit to the cavern
in some uncle's molar

*and woodchip craft at best)*
for who doesn't have chips
lying around

*and the obstacles were many.*
Just the beginning of problems
we'd create for ourselves.

*(A single stem, for example*
pointing to last year's growth
and subsequent death

*would divert the entire system*
solar and school, the stars
leaving us standing

*four inches left.) Boats made*
us feel beneath them.
That's not why we fuss about

*progress, though.*
Poke anything with a stick
and eventually it goes.

3.

*As for the culvert*
bringing to mind
me and my house

*we knew*
as kids from a certain time
tend to

*that by the time*
measured by our growling
stomachs

*we'd followed the stream*
the edges of our tracks
bulging with mud

*all the way from downtown*
giving only a quick eyes-down hi
to the few adults we snaked past

*to the last block*
a territory claimed
and never outgrown

*nudging our boats along*
as you would a friend
who has lost a love to another

*(at times they needed no help)*
after all some friends just shrug
you off and carry on

*to the Wiebes' house*
the door properly closed
the blinds

*half-way down* was,
like any journey, measured with a half-
way point.

*The fact that MY house was*
unlocked and not entirely mine
(though it was, wasn't it?)

*the last one before the culvert*
which glugged like anything
in a rush to find a way out

*complicated things a bit.*
The apparent thirst
unquenchable.

*The water got faster there*
our boats, not mine, our time
fleeting as it was

*and us more nervous.*
Already we could see ourselves
older and falling.

*Half the time we couldn't stop*
ourselves and had to construct
makeshift anchors to secure

*our boats but they were gone.*

4.

*Always another boat*
sometimes Huck's raft
sometimes a warship.

*Sometimes we'd run*
the fastest racing, the slow
pretending to be above it

*back to the top*
all set to follow
this slope down

*the official footwear*
not guaranteed to keep
feet warm

*on the four-block journey*
we'd map
our lives by

*from downtown*
(Not available locally. Growth
restrictions may apply)

*was the rubber boot*
the top two inches
folded down

*for extra speed.*
And could we ever fly
when we had to.

*In summer the culvert*
steel as hot as
nerves and tempers

*didn't seem so mean*
little tracks we couldn't identify
weaving between the pebbles

*just dried up.*
Every woodchip
a shipwrecked dream.

*Until it rained*
we always love
when it rains

*and the boats set sail*
anchorless again
our small lives

*and the culvert opened wide.*

## That Little Baby

*A few years ago we had to install one on a piece of property out west. Until then I really didn't understand their importance. Now we have conversations with neighbours about "how well the culvert's holding up."*

Just listen to the way it gurgles
contentedly in the sun, as if the sun

were cuddling it, its belly full
for now. Hours of contractions

long past. The slow, careful delivery
by expert hands and the flatbed

fade from memory. We often place hope
in a crib, back down, snuggly wrapped,

monitor it day and night, watch it grow
while we grow wary. We watch it latch

and latch this one did. Mouth wide, the whole
flood is sucked in, pours through. You bet

*we're very proud of that little baby.*
A miracle means change. Is always wet.

# Tracked Down

1.

*. . . a pal and I were scouting out the big culvert on the road west of the Catholic church. In it we found some obviously stolen goods which we tracked down to having been taken from Zander's store on Main Street (the little store in the middle of the block between the shoe store and Brownstone's). We returned the goods. Don't remember if there was a little reward but certainly a couple of twelve-year-old girls felt pretty noble as the Zanders were very appreciative.*

2.

I robbed my grandmother. I robbed from the rich and gave to the poor girl who really wanted another Kit Kat. I hid the evidence in the trees where I played, slicing the air with my stick sword and riding off to save the villagers, the chickens parting when they saw me galloping their way, red combs and wattles waving. Outlaws are revered as much as they are feared. All this was before I learned how to hide things well. Despite my noble deeds on behalf of the have-not, I was fingered as the prime suspect and tried. The case wrapped up quickly. I pleaded guilty and was sentenced to life without anything sweet.

## The West Side of the House

Midnight. The west side of the house. Let's say you came here to leave an impression, let's say you knew when to take it outside, when to lead the way through the brome grass. You've been to this empty place before. The crowd wants a story to remember. You borrow what you need: yarns that turn parties into dark quests few have the courage to face alone. Tonight you take the closest hand in yours and half the party follows like always, follows your story now as it grows and starts twigging. *My first memory is of falling into a hole a backhoe was digging,*

you say, your voice haunted, almost a whisper. Bull, says some guy. Someone throws a bottle. Others lean in, as if a supporting role will bring them fame, but your crowd is like that, drawn swearing and giggling into any little drama. They scream on the west side of the house for no reason, half lost in a wind from hell that just shows up at parties. Someone laughs. Tonight the story demands punch. A coyote howls. You howl back: I was found dead in a culvert *when I was three years old.*

And place your forehead against the siding, beat your fists against the wood, belt out your best "In the Air Tonight." What next, someone says. Bull, goes another. The crowd stares but you howl again, then turn to the wall. You practised for this. Someone cracks a beer as you beat the clapboard drum and the beer foams in the not-quite moonlight, a mouth caps off the flow, you lose the words, your hands no longer yours. Let's say the only words that come: above Chisolm's shoe store in Antigonish, Nova Scotia, *my mom* laid me to rest.

A shoe store, someone laughs. O please, when were you in Nova Scotia? A lighter flicks, flame to palm, smoke blowing in your face. This is when you walk away, holding on to no one, your fists wet commas at the end of your sleeves, cuffs undone as always. Let's say the crowd follows, the footfalls heavy. Are you alright? You've got them. They stop when you stop. You look back at the house, find a line in the siding. I'll be honest, you say. Being afraid *rescued me*. I remember *I was wearing a striped T-shirt, a bit frayed.*

# Ducks

*As we passed over the culverts my heart was in my mouth and I gripped the car door in panic.*

dumped
at the mouth of a culvert,
hundreds of yellow
plastic ducks enter the rush,
with red bills, wide eyes,
eyelashes each side
and away they go!
Corporate ducks racing
in top hats and chef hats,
hard hats and punk dos,
ducks sporting golf balls,
carrying lattes,
wearing camo, shades,
bearing nuts and screws,
ducks driving
airboats and houseboats,
wearing wedding veils,
ducks holding chocolate
wrapped in cellophane

secured with a thin burgundy
ribbon with gold script
tied in a perfect bow,
biker ducks in biker leathers,
ducks who will float aimlessly
out into the weed, washed up,
poked with sticks.
This is how children
learn to mind their business.

# Skunkdom

## 1.

*Skunks go in culverts. That's what they do.*

All my life I've been a world
unto myself, on my knees praying
for myself, the cat looking on.

Of course the cat understands
the reasoning. At least I hope
the cat understands. I don't

leave my room until an audience gathers
outside the door, which means I
don't leave my room anymore.

I just feel around and grab a coke
knowing the can is there. It gives
a measured hiss when I pull the tab.

2.

*Shot a skunk in one. Went fuckin' deaf for two hours. Got the skunk
though.*

All my life I've been a child
on my knees trying to retrieve
the cat from under the granary.

Of course the cat ran under there
for a reason, but I don't consider
the cat's choices or mine.

Like a member of an audience
called onto the stage to draw a raffle
ticket for a 50-50, I reach in,

feel around and grab what I can. The tail
feels thick, resistant. It makes no sense
until I pull it into the light.

## Culvert Triolet at Dawn with Blasting Cap and a Fuse

*One way to clean it is with dynamite. But then you don't have a road.*

One way to clean it is with dynamite
      But then you don't have a road
      to take through the valley at night
One way to clean it is with dynamite
Blast the wicked shit into the light
road be dammed
      Good god  What a load
One way to clean it is with dynamite
      But then you don't have a road

# I don't know what the hell a culvert is (no offence)

*I* said come here, you say
    but the dog enters the mouth.

*Don't* ignore me. You don't
    know what's in there. But dogs

*know.* Her tail brushes the steel
    and she's gone, no matter

*what* you say, what you yell.
    Come out of there!

*the* call not enough to bring the dog
    out of the specific

*hell* she's walked into, the panting
    so loud before she reappears you fear

*a* change you can't name
    has occurred. Later the word

*culvert* comes out of a stranger's
    mouth. The dog

*is* not there to hear, but you
    wonder if she understood

*no* way, you think, but you picture
    her looking back and

*(offence)* seeing the shape
    your lips took at the beginning.

# Regarding the Handout Photo of the Boy under the Headline

*Hutterite boy awakens from coma, wonders about fuss*
— *Winnipeg Free Press*

Sucked into a culvert, the story says.
Under ice the colour of his eyes
his lungs filled, his heart quit, a phase
he doesn't remember. No surprise

the flood waters that claimed him
after twenty minutes let him go,
that it took another two weeks for him
to let go of the spring, the melted snow

melting away a consciousness unknown
to most of us. He took in mayflies, seeds,
the promise caught in the intake and drowned
in outpourings. His pupils are elegies

side by side beneath the road's surface,
passages into which the works will race.

# It: Bears Repeating

*Is that a bear? No. Is that a bear? No. Is that a bear?*

A pronoun. I [1] Subjective uses.

## 1 *The inanimate or abstract thing*

Is that a bear? No. Two bears, that's what it is, almost touching on the shadow side of the road. A friend once told me she asks this over and over during road trips up here, and it's true, at a distance bears and large culverts look the same. From the car, though, the bears are the size of floaters and move with the same randomness when I blink. Floaters appear more often in my field of vision nowadays, something to do with aging and the shrinking of the vitreous humour. H stops the car. I begin shooting as photographers do when they find a subject.

## 2 *The subject of thought*

Something is hanging from one bear's mouth. A cub? No. Too small. Whatever it is, I know by the limpness, the darkness, that it's not alive, or if it is, it will not be alive for long.

---

[1] The senses in this piece are adapted from the entry for 'it' found in the *Shorter Oxford English Dictionary*.

### 3 *As subject of an impersonal verb without reference*

It being spring, we are drawn to the backroads, occupied with any movement in the shadows. Grouse lost in the dappled light, their chicks lost behind lumps the grader leaves along the edge of any backroad. Sometimes we see a bear, sometimes a bear with cubs, but never two adults. Adult bears are solitary. But it's June 1, the early days of mating season. The North American Bear Centre website says male black bears have a mating range ten to fifteen miles in diameter; the range, rich with scent trails, contains the territories of seven to fifteen females and, I might add, one to two photographers with no sense at all.

### 4 *As anticipatory subject*

We creep forward — does it make a difference how quickly we approach? It excites me, the prospect of seeing the two (or three?) interact, the prospect of capturing evidence, but I know from past experience how quickly and completely a bear can disappear. It can be gone like that. Surely two will disappear doubly fast.

II *Objective uses*

5 *The thing etc*

The bears fold as one, left over right, into the light. They've reached the clearing. We passed by the place yesterday, as we have so many times over the past thirty years, and paused to take it in, hoping to spot something. It is lush, all manner of greens, some waist high, some chest high, most of which I can't name, but it's the type of place you find bears grazing. Now is our chance and, given the state of things, it may be our last chance. H wants to move south as soon as we can. I don't, but I'm beginning to accept it, the logic, not that logic will help me deal with the loss. Hurry, I say. H accelerates. I check the lens for dirt, I check the settings.

6 *Vague or indefinite object of a verb*

Make it up as you go, some say of life, though nowadays it's more of a shoot-it-up-and-post-it approach, and this is the very approach I use when I photograph anything that's moving. It means I try to be prepared for the briefest of opportunities. Today I am. The vibration reduction is on. The heavy lens is resting on the window. I shoot in RAW. I will take hundreds of photos so that I can answer the doubters with proof. I've been questioned before and I will certainly be questioned about this. The sun hits me as we pause in the clearing. I squint. A bear raises its head. Drops what it is holding. It stops chewing. It's frowning, I say to H as I shoot. With that the bear is gone.

III *7 Antecedent to a relative expressed*

The frown: full face, about face, facing valleys of hot fur and no end of bugs, facing a lifetime of disappointment. Is it not *it* that has cut into the forest?

I sit back. I've lived over half a century. I'm old enough to know how to project, how to wait for it to return. I know it will. And it does. But wait: this is the other.

IV *8 Now colloquial*

They don't do it. Not in front of us. But I can feel the tension between them. I know the tension. It raises the scruff on the other one's neck. It makes the other one close in on our position and lie down. It appears most nonchalant, non-threatening, grazing silently in the Eden-like beauty of the late afternoon, the lulling rhythm of its jaws beckoning us to approach. Enter our clearing, it seems to say. Enter our circle. Cross the threshold of light.

*9 The acme*

Teeth flash. It stands up. That's it. Let's go, I say, but H says, No, keep shooting. You're safe, he says. I recall the story of the bear attack in Saskatchewan this spring; picture the bandaged leg of the woman from Paradise Hill, the spot of blood that has leaked through the dressing and through the layers of gauze that hold it in place. Keep shooting, he says. It can't get you, he says. But it has. It has my fear between its teeth and it's grinding.

*10 Sex appeal*

The loping bear has a certain "it." It comes to a stop, sits down, and scowls the whole time it eats. It gets up and tears a chunk out of the earth. The standing bear returns to all fours, but I don't notice it making its way until it's nearly there. How can I not sense all that weight leaving?


## 11 *In predicate use: the player*

It stands on its hind legs, a nightmare, but faces away. It seems I no longer matter. Maybe I never did. I don't believe the adage that women, when they reach a certain age, become invisible, but why does that saying occur to me now? A breeze brushes my cheek as I shoot. A darkness enters the clearing on the right, lopes counter-clockwise around the periphery without making a single sound.


## B *Possessive adjective*

Its nose reaches out. It reaches like it did before when sniffing us out. But I was wrong about that like I am about so many things. I am not that perceptive. Is scowling bear receptive? On the edge of the clearing I believe they fold once again into a single mass, but I cannot focus. Something is in the way.

## To Catch a Culvert Thief

*Thieves haul away 12-metre-long culvert*
*— CBC News Saskatchewan*

You need a culvert thief, a copycat.
The Culvert, we'll call him. Or her. You see

culverts are jewels in these parts. Yes, the plot
structure has been covered. No Grace Kelly

in this version and no happy ending
has been reported. This is a story

ditched by the producer overspending
not the culprit. The hitch? There's no glory

in catching the difference between steel and steal,
subtle as it is on the tongue. One shines

the ear, the other covers it. Big deal,
you say as the getaway semi whines,

here we're galvanized, gauged, corrosiveness
not a problem. Here. Bury the witness.

# Culvert FAQ

*1. Have you ever seen a culvert ripped from its resting place deformed and mangled?*

Yes. It looks like a woolly bear curled up where the fingers meet the palm.

*2. There was a four-foot plank bridge about three feet from the culvert?*

Yes. Someone played there and when she *heard* her *mom call* her *full name,* she *knew it was time to head home without delay.*

3. Do you know someone who knows someone who lived beside someone who kept a maze of culverts in the backyard through which he made salamanders crawl?

Yes. The story is educational. It's been recorded and is safe.

4. Can historic stone culverts be excavated and installed inside a home?

Yes. I sat beside a conductor who had sat before such a hearth in France and I felt the warmth.

5. Was Gadhafi killed in or near a culvert?

Yes. He'd been hiding in the belly of a culvert amidst graffiti. Pro tip: Do not google on a full stomach.


6. *We were down in the bottom shooting muskrats. Heard a vehicle coming and poof it hit the ditch. It hit the approach, hit the culvert and buggered up the wheel. It was undrivable after that?*

Yes.


7. In the 1960s, were concrete culverts big enough to allow Audrey Hepburn and Albert Finney to sit up or lie down in comfort?

Yes. Watch *Two for the Road*. Then watch it again.